Jan Stanley

If I Could Breathe Like Fishes Do

Illustrator
Ron Wennekes

ISBN 0-9776893-0-1

Copyright @2006 by Jan Stanley

Printed by Midwest Graphics, Chicago, Illinois 60606

To Trevor, Jennifer and Kyle, may you always retain your sense of curiosity and wonder at the world that's around you.

My heartfelt thanks to everyone who worked to bring these little fish to life, but most especially to my dear friend Jane. You make beautiful magic.

If I could breathe like fishes do, I'd dance upon the beach
and know that stars beneath the waves are well within my reach.

I'd swim the deep in search of things not found upon the shore.
The angel, box and parrotfish would help me to explore.

Perhaps I'd glide below the waves upon a turtle's shell
and learn the language dolphins speak
and hear the tales they tell.

If I could breathe like fishes do, I'd go to marlin school
and learn the things fishes teach about the golden rule.

From flying fish and albatross, to seals and manatees,
abalone, cod and eel, I'd study all of these.

While swimming 'round a coral reef, I'd view the diners there,
and use an urchin's spiny back to comb a mermaid's hair.

I'd float beneath the salty waves and spy the toothy shark
and there I'd find the truth about if dogfish really bark.

If I saw a butterfly fish while swimming in the seas,
I'd wonder how it likes it there with currents for a breeze.

If I found a sunken ship now crewed by albacore,
 I'd join their merry band to sail the seven seas once more.

We'd play our favorite pirate games with swordfish as our foe,
Or watch the clown and lionfish in a deep-seas circus show.

If I could breathe like fishes do, I'd swim with humpback whales and stick my feet up in the air just like they do their tails.

I'd listen to the whales' song and imitate their notes,
and maybe find Atlantis lost, way down below the boats.

I'd play baseball with an octopus, but I'd have to swim quite fast.

You see, he has eight arms for throwing and his skill is unsurpassed.

I could use the waving kelp strands as a place to hide-n-seek.
 I think I'd play the game with minnows,
  even though they sometimes peek.

I wonder if a trumpet fish can hit the highest notes,
 and do squirrelfish look like squirrels, and do goatfish look like goats?

I'd like to know if surgeonfish help fishes that are hurt.
Do garden eels need more water with their tails stuck in the dirt?

If I could breathe like fishes do, I'd never leave the deep.
I'd hunt among the oyster beds to find a place to sleep.

And as the day was ending, I would lay my sleepy head
on a pillow made of sponges, with a clamshell for my bed.

About the Author

The mother of three grown children, Jan Stanley lives in Spokane, Washington with her husband and two dogs. She was born on a sprawling ranch in central Montana, and was fifth in a family of eleven children. Her love of animals and her vivid imagination are traits that were nourished by her parents.

Jan's hope is that the children who read her book will know the simple joy of allowing their imagination to run free. Always hungering to know just a little more. Never afraid to be different or try something new. Her belief is that this journey to know, explore and understand often begins with the question "What if?"

Imagine!

Jan Stanley
12/'05